28th

Paul

GU00862654

Love One Another

(John 13:34)

A personal look at the reality of the urgent search for Christian unity

Charles Whitehead

May the Lord bless you and guide you,

Charles

The illustration on the front cover is taken from a banner produced by Yvonne Bell in 2005 for the CELEBRATE Conference
Yvonnebell@yvonnebell.co.uk

In the words of Pope Benedict XVI,
**'Ecumenism is absolutely central
to the Christian Life.'**

FOREWORD

T HIS BOOKLET IS A TIMELY PRESENTATION of the importance for all Christians of the search for Christian Unity. The divisions and separations in the Christian world are an anomaly. There have of course been significant advances in the search for 'full communion' between Christians in recent times but those developments put the outstanding differences into even clearer relief.

Charles Whiteheads' commitment to Christian Unity has been shaped by many factors but especially by his being married to an Anglican and by the vital role he has played in the Catholic Charismatic Renewal. Important here is a recurring theme in Pope Francis' teaching about the Catholic Charismatic Renewal, namely that it is an 'ecumenical grace' - a grace that does not recognise ecclesiastical boundaries.

In this booklet Charles reminds us of some of the Church's key teachings about ecumenism, and reading through them one has to wonder how much this teaching has really been appreciated and implemented and how much it actually shapes Catholic life, prayer and ministry.

So this book is also a timely reminder to all Christians of who and what we are and of what we are called and gifted to become.

+Kevin McDonald
Archbishop Emeritus of Southwark

1

INTRODUCTION

MY OWN COMMITMENT TO CHRISTIAN UNITY began in 1976, when my Anglican wife, Sue, and I were both inspired by the powerful witness of some Anglican and Baptist friends, to the presence and work of the Holy Spirit in their lives. Suffice it to say that we both came to a living faith, Sue from some years of atheism.

We both experienced a new outpouring of the Holy Spirit, and began working enthusiastically for the spread of the Gospel. For 30 years we held a weekly ecumenical prayer meeting in our home and over time we have given talks at conferences and churches of different traditions all over the world. We have both written Christian books, have initiated and organised conferences together, whilst remaining part of our respective Anglican and Catholic Churches.

I have personally chaired and co-chaired a good number of Catholic and Ecumenical local, national and international organisations and events, and for ten years had the use of an office in the Vatican with regular meetings with Pope John Paul II. A particular part of my work has been building close relationships with Pentecostals and leaders of the new Independent Charismatic Churches and Fellowships.

In all of this, over more than forty years, the desire to see an ever-increasing unity throughout the whole body of Christ, locally, nationally and internationally, has remained of paramount importance. For any of us this will normally begin with the building of strong personal relationships with our Christian brothers and sisters from other traditions in the area where we live. Little of substance will happen ecumenically until these friendships are in place, but once they are, the Lord will start to do some amazing things.

I have written this booklet mainly for Catholics, with the simple aim of presenting some of the exciting Church teaching and encouragement to us to work for unity throughout the universal body of Christ. I hope you will find it helpful and challenging, and that it will result in a greatly increased desire to build new relationships with all our brothers and sisters in Christ.

Charles Whitehead

LOVE ONE ANOTHER
Spiritual and Receptive
Ecumenism

Brothers and sisters in Christ

Ecumenism, the search for Christian unity, has assumed much greater importance for many Christians in recent years. There are a number of reasons for this, foremost among which is usually considered to be the accelerating decline in Western Christianity resulting from the relentless advance of materialism and consumerism. In other words, the decline in numbers in many denominations forces us to recognise that we need each other if we are to maintain any influence in our respective countries. Another reason is the steady rise of other faiths, accelerated by the threat posed by terrorism both nationally and internationally.

Whilst factors like these are important, we must also believe that awareness of the prayer of Jesus in **John 17** that his followers might be one '**so that the world may believe that you have sent me**' (vs. 21) is growing, and that relationships between local and national Christian leaders are improving, inspired by the friendships of **Pope Francis, Archbishop Justin Welby** and others. Whatever the reasons may be, the growing interest in developing good relations with all our brothers and sisters in Christ is something in which we are all called to play our part. This is the reason I have written this short booklet, aimed mainly, but not exclusively, at a Catholic readership and designed to offer a pastoral and theological framework for our important work towards greater

Christian unity. In the words of the late Cardinal Suenens 'true ecumenism is coming together, not as we are, but as we should be'.

TOGETHER WE'VE GOT IT!

We are all on a journey and we have not yet arrived, and whilst none of us have got it together, together we've got it! Paul writing to the Corinthian Church appealed for unity: '**I do appeal to you brothers, for the sake of Our Lord Jesus Christ, to make up the differences between you and instead of disagreeing among yourselves, be united again in your belief and practices**' 1 Corinthians 1:10-17.

MY PERSONAL CALLING

My involvement in this whole area has been considerable over the last 40 years. My wife, Sue, is a committed Anglican and I am Catholic. When we both came to a living faith in 1976, the Lord clearly told each of us to '**bloom where you were planted**' and so that is what we try to do. But of course part of it is to work together for unity throughout the body of Christ. More details of our joint and extensive ecumenical work is given at the end of this booklet. All this, and more, is work to which I feel the Lord has called me and where we have seen very good progress in developing mutual understanding, trust, respect, and co-operation. So my hope is that this short booklet will be helpful in putting the Church's commitment to Christian unity into context, and will provide encouragement and a sense of purpose for anyone who is questioning the value of giving their time and effort to building closer relationships with all their brothers and sisters in Christ in the other parts of His body.

A BRIEF HISTORY

The Catholic Church's approach to ecumenism has changed out of all recognition in my lifetime. As I write this, in the papacy of **Francis**, the pace of change is accelerating all the time. To help us appreciate the significance of what we are living through, a brief look at the history of ecumenism will provide an important context for these reflections.

It was very clear in the first half of the twentieth century that the Church felt it was essential to emphasise the risks involved in ecumenism and to actively discourage it. During the pontificate of **Pope Pius XI** it was clearly stated in 1928 in a papal letter entitled '**Mortalium Animos**', that it was fundamentally wrong to pray with other Christians. 'Intrinsically evil' was the emotive phrase used. Not surprisingly the embryonic ecumenical movement was condemned and stifled, and such was the deep-rooted hostility that any relationships with Christians of other traditions were strongly disapproved of. This very negative attitude prevailed into the 1940s, as I know from two personal examples.

A 'MIXED' MARRIAGE

My parents were married in January 1942 during World War II in a Catholic Church in Rhyl, North Wales. My mother was a staunch Catholic from an Irish background and my father a middle-of-the-road Anglican. Officially music, flowers and a wedding dress for my mother were banned as a sign that the Church accepted but did not fully approve of this 'mixed' marriage. In fact it just so happened that the choir was practising wedding music that Saturday morning, the flower arranger had come in early to set out the flowers for Sunday, and the long white dress was not officially described by my mother's dressmaker as 'a wedding dress'!

'IT'S ALL VERY CONFUSING!'

When I started school in September 1947 at the age of almost five, there was no Catholic primary locally, so I was enrolled in the

Anglican school very close to where we lived. The Sunday before my first school day, our parish priest, Fr. Mooney, came for tea to explain that I was to leave the morning assembly when it came time for the prayers and to wait outside the door until they finished singing the hymn that concluded morning prayer. As I understood it, the Pope had told Fr. Mooney that I must never say prayers with Protestants, so I duly obeyed my instructions! Just over a year later, Fr. Mooney came for Sunday afternoon tea again to tell me that I could now stay in the morning assembly for the prayers, provided I did not say **'the funny bit'** at the end of the Our Father. My friends could not understand the sudden change, and I remember one of them telling me that if I didn't go out I'd probably go to hell! As we walked to our classrooms after the assembly, my teacher Miss Hughes, a good Welsh 'chapel' Christian, took me by the hand and asked me what was going on as she was very confused. I explained that the Pope had sent Fr. Mooney to tell me I could now stay for the prayers, to which she replied **'Well, I wish your Pope would make his mind up, it's all very confusing for the rest of us!'** What had really happened was that in 1949 a statement had come from the Vatican to say that **'the growing desire for unity is under the Holy Spirit'**, so prayer together was now to be encouraged. This was the beginning of a move forward in the whole area of our relationships with our **'separated brethren'** but it wasn't until the **Second Vatican Council** that the Church adopted a completely new, many would say revolutionary, approach to ecumenism.

PIONEERS IN CHRISTIAN UNITY

For quite some years before **Pope Saint John XXIII** called the **Second Vatican Council** in 1962, there had been a few gentle signs of a new desire for unity among some in the Church. The ecumenical pioneers who inspired this desire were men and women who were graced by the Lord to see what was wrong in what everyone else was taking for granted – the existence of separate, competing and often antagonistic Christian Churches and Fellowships. These pioneers were prophetic figures who had the courage to stand up and say what they believed was God's view of the squabbling, bitterness and negativity which was typical of the wider Christian community at the time.

One of them was **Abbé Paul Couturier** (1881-1953) from Lyon, France. He was ordained in 1904 and when helping to serve the refugees coming into France from the Russian Revolution was deeply moved by the piety of these Russian Orthodox Christians and saddened that it was not possible to share the Eucharist with them. He began to see how Catholics, Orthodox and Protestants all had painful memories of suffering at each other's hands, and he recognised that the only solution was repentance. In the mid 1930s he launched the **Week of Prayer for Christian Unity** from January 18th to 25th each year. It was Paul Couturier who opposed all talk of a 'return' and spoke instead of the '**restoration**' of Christian unity. The Vatican Council later accepted his view and regularly spoke of 'restoration' or 'reintegration', not of 'return'.

Another pioneer was **Max Josef Metzger** (1887-1944) from the Black Forest in Germany. Ordained in 1911, he served as a chaplain in World War I and was shattered by the horrors and suffering he experienced. So with two other priests in 1916 he founded a new religious order '**The World Peace League of the White Cross**'. As a result of his meetings with many Protestant Christians, he attended the Protestant '**Faith and Order Conference**' in 1927 as an official observer, and experienced a growing desire for unity among Christians. Like Couturier he recognised that the biggest blockages to unity were arrogance, pride, complacency, and a lack of love. He wrote letters to Pope Pius XII and to the Lutheran

Archbishop of Uppsala, Sweden, about peace and unity, but was arrested by the Nazis and tragically executed in 1944.

A third pioneer was **Blessed Maria Gabriella Sagheddu** (1914-1939) from Sardinia. In 1935 she entered the **Cistercian** convent in Grottaferrata, where the Lord began to impress upon her the importance of unity – with Him and among her sisters. During the Week of Prayer for Christian Unity in 1937, she read a letter from Abbé **Paul Couturier** about the unity of all Christians and offered her life to the Lord for this cause. She died of tuberculosis in 1939 and after her death the pages of **John 17** were found, yellowed and worn, as they had been her daily meditation. She was beatified by **Pope Saint John Paul II** in 1983 and held up as a model of spiritual ecumenism. She is the **Patron of the Ecumenical Movement**.

Other pioneers include **Dom Lambert Beaudouin** (1873-1960) who founded a monastery dedicated to prayer for Christian unity; **Cardinal Mercier** (1856-1926) who hosted the **Malines Conversations** with the Anglicans; and **Cardinal Johannes Willebrands** who brought the early Catholic pioneers together. In much more recent times, the 1970s and 1980s, **Cardinal Leon-Josef Suenens** strongly encouraged the **Catholic Charismatic Renewal** in its ecumenical endeavors, asserting that the **Renewal** was ecumenical by its very nature.

So we were starting to move forward in the whole area of relationships with our **'separated brethren'**, but it was when the Vatican Council members started discussing ecumenism in 1963 that a completely new approach was born - **Unitatis Redintegratio**, The Restoration of Unity.

EXTRACTS FROM 'UNITATIS REDINTEGRATIO' – VATICAN II 1964

If we now look in detail at some parts of **Unitatis Redintegratio**, the Vatican II Decree on Ecumenism published in 1964, we will have a much clearer picture of what the Church gave us as the launching pad for modern ecumenical practice. I will simply put forward a series of selected statements taken from the document which express and make clear the mind of the Fathers of the Council on this subject. **This is not going to be light and easy reading, but I encourage you to persevere because here we find some key teaching on Christian unity.**

The very first sentence contains a definitive statement:-
'The restoration of unity among all Christians is one of the principal concerns of the Second Vatican Council.' In the first paragraph we are also reminded that:- *'Division openly contradicts the will of Christ, scandalises the world, and damages the holy cause of preaching the Gospel to every creature'.*

FROM SECTION 3
EARLY SIGNS OF DIVISION
'Even in the beginnings of this one and only Church of God there arose certain rifts. But in subsequent centuries much more serious dissensions made their appearance and quite large communities came to be separated from full communion with the Catholic Church – for which, often enough, men of both sides were to blame'.

'The children who are born into these communities and who grow up believing in Christ cannot be accused of the sin involved in the separation, and the Catholic Church embraces them as brothers and sisters with respect and affection. For those who believe in Christ and have been truly baptised are in communion with the Catholic Church even though this communion is imperfect'.

JUSTIFICATION BY FAITH IN BAPTISM

'But in spite of the obstacles it remains true that all who have been justified by faith in Baptism are members of Christ's body and have a right to be called Christian, and so are correctly accepted as brothers and sisters by the children of the Catholic Church'.

'The separated Churches and Communities as such, though we believe them to be deficient in some respects, have been by no means deprived of significance and importance in the mystery of salvation. For the Spirit of Christ has not refrained from using them as means of salvation which derive their efficacy from the very fullness of grace and truth entrusted to the Church'.

Having laid a framework of justification for a new commitment to working for unity, the Council Fathers then encouraged all Catholics to become actively involved, as we now see in Section 4 of the document.

FROM SECTION 4
ACTIVE ECUMENISM

'The Sacred Council exhorts all the Catholic faithful to recognise the signs of the times and to take an active and intelligent part in the work of ecumenism'.

'.......avoid expressions, judgements and actions which do not represent the condition of our separated brethren with truth and fairness'.

THE IMPORTANCE OF DIALOGUE AND PRAYER

'In dialogue everyone gains a truer knowledge and more just appreciation of the teaching and life of both Communions. In addition, the way is prepared for co-operation between them in the

duties for the common good of humanity which are demanded by every Christian conscience; and wherever this is allowed, there is prayer in common. Finally, all are led to examine their own faithfulness to Christ's will for the Church and accordingly to undertake with vigour the task of renewal and reform'.

The document goes on to make clear that while we remain assured that the Catholic Church has the fullest understanding of the message of salvation, this does not mean we are living this out as clearly as we should. Catholics must also recognise and value the gifts which are found among brothers and sisters in other Churches and Fellowships.

'Catholics, in their ecumenical work, must assuredly be concerned for their separated brethren, praying for them, keeping them informed about the Church, making the first approaches toward them.'

'Although the Catholic Church has been endowed with all divinely revealed truth and with all the means of grace, yet its members fail to live by them with all the fervor they should, so that the radiance of the Church's image is less clear in the eyes of our separated brethren and of the world at large, and the growth of God's kingdom is delayed.'

FREEDOM IN THE SPIRITUAL LIFE
'All in the Church must preserve unity in essentials. But let all, according to the gifts they have received, enjoy a proper freedom in their various forms of spiritual life and discipline, in their various liturgical rites, and even in their theological elaborations of revealed truth.'

'On the other hand, Catholics must gladly acknowledge and esteem

*the truly Christian endowments from our common heritage which
are to be found among our separated brethren.'*

My Purpose Here

My purpose in offering here a variety of quotations from **Unitatis
Redintegratio** is simply to give you some examples of the
remarkable statements included in the Document in the hope that
you will be stimulated into obtaining a copy and studying it for
yourself. So rather than continue to offer too many quotations, here
in conclusion of this part are just a few from sections 7 to 9
inclusive.

From Section 7
Prayer to the Holy Spirit

*'There can be no ecumenism worthy of the name without a change
of heart.........We should therefore pray to the Holy Spirit for the
grace to be genuinely self-denying, humble, gentle in the service of
others, and to have an attitude of brotherly generosity towards
them.'*

From Section 8
Spiritual Ecumenism and Prayer Together

*'......change of heart and holiness of life, along with public and
private prayer for the unity of Christians, should be regarded as
the soul of the whole ecumenical movement, and merits the name
'spiritual ecumenism.' '*

*'......it is allowable, indeed desirable, that Catholics should join
in prayer with their separated brethren. Such prayers in common
are certainly an effective means of obtaining the grace of unity and
they are a true expression of the ties which still bind Catholics to
their separated brethren.'*

FROM SECTION 9
'We must get to know the outlook of our separated brethren.'

SUMMARY
In sections 13 to 18, **Unitatis Redintegratio** goes on to look in more detail at unity with the Eastern Churches, and in sections 19 to 23 at unity with the separated Churches and Ecclesial Communities in the West. All these sections are important and well worth reading, but they need quiet personal study and reflection. My purpose in this booklet is simply to highlight some key statements to stimulate an increasing interest in the work for Christian unity.

SOME COMMENTS ON VATICAN II AND ECUMENISM TODAY
We know how important the **Second Vatican Council** was in presenting the Church with a challenging vision for the way ahead on many fronts, and we also know it was not well received by everyone. Elderly people in particular found the changes hard to accept. My very committed and faithful Catholic grandmother, a Third Order Franciscan, never really came to terms with the Mass in English and the priest facing the people. Then there are things decided by the Council which are yet to be fully implemented, but it's clear that Pope Francis intends to do whatever he can to make sure this happens.

In his Apostolic Exhortation '**Evangelii Gaudium**' he lays out his own vision and desire to move the entire Church from a '**maintenance**' to a '**missionary**' mentality: '**Mere administration can no longer be enough. Throughout the world let us be permanently in a state of mission' (section 25)**. He also strongly supports the building of close relationships with our brothers and sisters in other parts of the body of Christ. Francis clearly identifies all who have accepted Jesus Christ as their Lord and Saviour as our brothers and sisters in Him. We'll be looking more closely at this later on. In many different areas he's also challenging our self-understanding as Catholics and calling us to proclaim the Gospel with joy and passion! Is he a reformer, a revolutionary, or does he just have a simple agenda for radical renewal and re-building of the Church? He's not afraid to challenge us!

POPE SAINT JOHN XXIII – A RADICAL REFORMER

It's often been said that when Pope John XXIII was elected, the College of Cardinals believed they were choosing an elderly man who would just keep things ticking over for a few years. How wrong they were! The man they elected turned out to be one of the most radical reformers in Church history. His decision to call the Second Vatican Council took everyone by surprise, and he played a very active role in the preparations to ensure that the final **lineamenta** encapsulated his vision for the modern Church which he was determined would become better equipped to present the Gospel to the world of the second half of the twentieth century and on into the 21st.

So the **Second Vatican Council** (1962-1965) was an historic turning point for the Catholic Church. As we have already seen, one change of momentous significance was the Church's softened and increasingly positive attitude towards the other Christian Churches and Ecclesial Communities. From a previous position of clear-cut separation and often aggressive argument, the bishops voted overwhelmingly for much more positive relationships with other Christians in the 1964 Decree on Ecumenism. Church divisions were seen as contradicting the will of Christ and, for the first time, as scandalising the world. **Pope Saint John XXIII** was determined to put Christian unity firmly on the map and into the teaching of the Council. The resulting Decree on Ecumenism was strongly criticised and even rejected by many of those opposed to the whole approach of Vatican II, who claimed that it brought discontinuity into the teaching of the Church in a number of areas, of which unity was one. It certainly represented a major shift in Catholic teaching.

As Pope Benedict explained it to the Roman Curia on December 22nd 2005:- '**The Second Vatican Council with its new definition of the relationship between the faith of the Church and certain elements of modern thought, has reviewed or even corrected certain historical decisions, and in this apparent discontinuity, it has actually preserved and deepened her inmost nature and identity'**.

AUTHENTIC FAITH IN OTHER CHURCHES
All Catholics brought up before Vatican II were taught that the Catholic Church was the one true Church, the One, Holy, Catholic and Apostolic Church of the Nicene Creed. Attitudes towards other Christians were logical deductions from that position. If the Catholic Church is the one true Church, then all the others must be false churches. This was the issue the Council Fathers tackled.

THE ROMAN CATHOLIC CHURCH WAS UNIQUE, BUT…
They believed that the Roman Catholic Church was unique and not just one among many. But they also recognised authentic faith in Jesus Christ and the presence of the Holy Spirit in other churches too. This meant they had to clarify the relationship of the Catholic Church to the other Christian churches.

CATHOLICS ARE NOT BETTER THAN OTHER CHRISTIANS
They noted the basis for the uniqueness of the Catholic Church, as through this Church alone '**can the fullness of the means of salvation' be obtained (Unitatis Redintegratio section 3)**. But they also indicated that this uniqueness did not mean Catholics are

better than other Christians (section 4). Nor does it mean that Catholics have made the best use of this fullness of the means of salvation. Other Christians may have received more life from God through fewer means of grace. Christians of other denominations are not outsiders like pagans are. They are within, although imperfectly within. Therefore none of us can treat Protestant Christians as if they don't belong to the Church of Jesus Christ. '**The Spirit of Christ has not refrained from using them as means of salvation' (section 3).**

THE CATHOLIC CATECHISM AND OTHER STATEMENTS

Another valuable source to help us appreciate and improve our understanding of Church teaching on unity is the **Catechism of the Catholic Church**. There we find that Section 818 reminds us again: '**All who have been justified by faith in Baptism are incorporated into Christ; they therefore have a right to be called Christians and with good reason are accepted as brothers and sisters in the Lord by the Catholic Church'**. This acceptance is the starting point for the development of positive ecumenical relations.

UNITY OF THE SPIRIT IN THE BOND OF PEACE

In any natural family there are often disagreements between parents and children, brothers and sisters, fathers and sons, mothers and daughters, but the family relationship is still there – it is not destroyed by the disagreements. So it is between brothers and sisters in Christ. We are all - **Catholic, Protestant, Independent, Orthodox, Pentecostal** - adopted into Christ, and adoption gives us all full and equal position and rights. Chapter one of Paul's letter to the **Ephesians** reminds them and us all that we have been **chosen, adopted, redeemed, claimed, paid for, forgiven, and blessed**. In chapter 4 we are exhorted to '**preserve the unity of the Spirit in the bond of peace'** and reminded that there is: '**One Body,** one Spirit, one Hope, one Lord, one Faith, one Baptism, one God and Father of all who is over all and through all and in all' (Ephesians 4:4). So our unity is not just an abstract concept – it means being together and doing things together so that we can say with the psalmist 'How good, how delightful it is for all to live together as brothers' (Psalm 133).

THE ECUMENICAL VENTURE

Of course we can sit back, believing that the fullness of Divine Revelation subsists in the Catholic Church, so we'll just wait for everyone else to see the light and join or re-join us. But this attitude means we are setting ourselves above and completely ignoring what the Church is teaching us today about the journey towards Christian Unity – the 'ecumenical venture' to which she has made an 'irrevocable commitment'. We need to read what the Church is teaching us and to do what the Church is asking us – to be pro-active, and in this booklet I hope to remind us of the importance of all this.

OUR HOPE IS IN GOD

In Section 822 of the Catechism we are told: 'Concern for achieving unity involves the whole Church, faithful and clergy alike'. But we must realise 'That this holy objective – the reconciliation of all Christians in the unity of the one Church of Christ – transcends human gifts and powers'. That is why we place all our hope 'in the prayer of Christ for the Church, in the love of the Father for us, and in the power of the Holy Spirit'.

THE REQUIREMENTS FOR OUR RESPONSE

The Catechism section 821 lists the requirements for our response:
1. **Renewal** – for greater fidelity to our vocation.
2. **Conversion of heart** – for holier lives.

3. **Prayer in common** – 'spiritual ecumenism'.
4. **Fraternal knowledge** of each other.
5. **Dialogue and meetings**.
6. **Collaboration** in human service.

YOUCAT 131 TELLS US:

'Christian unity is the business of all Christians regardless of how young or old they are. Unity was one of Jesus' most important concerns (John 17:21). Divisions are like wounds on the body of Christ – they hurt and fester. Divisions lead to enmities and weaken the faith and credibility of Christians. Overcoming the scandal of separation requires the conversion of all concerned but also knowledge of one's own faith convictions, dialogue with others, and especially prayer in common and collaboration in serving mankind. Those in authority in the Church must not let the theological dialogue be interrupted.'

In *Tertio Millennio Adveniente*, section 16, Pope Saint John Paul II reminded us: '*Among the most fervent petitions which the Church makes to the Lord during this important time as the new millennium approaches, is that unity among all Christians of the various confessions will increase until they reach full communion.*'

In his own Encyclical Letter '*Ut Unum Sint*' section 4 he stated: '*I carry out this duty with the profound conviction that I am obeying the Lord, and with a clear sense of my own weakness.*'

'ECUMENISM IS ABSOLUTELY CENTRAL
TO THE CHRISTIAN LIFE'
Following his election as **Pope, Benedict XVI** told us that rebuilding the full and visible unity of all Christ's followers was his primary task. He said it was clear that '**for Catholics,**

ecumenism is absolutely central to the Christian life, both in terms of the Church becoming who she is and in terms of the Church's mission.' He said that in the end, each and every Christian must come before Christ and 'render an account to him of all we have done or failed to do to further the great good of the full and visible unity of all his disciples.'

PILGRIMS JOURNEYING TOGETHER
Then in **EVANGELII GAUDIUM sections 244-246**, Pope Francis points out: 'We must never forget that we are pilgrims journeying alongside each other. This means we must have sincere trust in our fellow pilgrims, putting aside all suspicion or mistrust and turn our gaze to what we are all seeking: the radiant peace of God's face.'

THE URGENCY OF SEEKING UNITY
'Given the seriousness of the counter-witness of division among Christians, particularly in Asia and Africa, the search for paths to unity becomes all the more urgent. Missionaries on those continents often mention the criticisms, complaints, and the ridicule to which the scandal of divided Christians gives rise. If we concentrate on the convictions we share and keep in mind the hierarchy of truths, we will be able to progress decidedly towards common expressions of proclamation, service and witness.'

AN EXCHANGE OF GIFTS
'If we really believe in the abundantly free working of the Holy Spirit, we can learn so much from one another! It is not just about being better informed about others, but rather about reaping what the Spirit has sown in them, which is also meant to be a gift for us. Through an exchange of gifts, the Spirit can lead us ever more fully into truth and goodness.'

UT UNUM SINT – the Encyclical Letter of Pope Saint John Paul II written in 1995 is another important document. To refer back to this Letter, here is a summary of the main content in which there are frequent quotations from **Unitatis Redintegratio**.

- At the Second Vatican Council, the Catholic Church committed herself irrevocably to following the path of ecumenical venture (section 3).
- This Sacred Synod (Vatican II) exhorts all the Catholic faithful to recognise the signs of the times and to participate actively in the work of ecumenism (section 8).
- We are brothers and sisters in Christ through our common Baptism (section 13).
- There is a need for renewal and personal conversion (section 15).
- Ecumenism is an organic part of the Church's life and work (section 20).
- What unites us is much greater than what divides us (section 21).
- Pray together – 'when Christians pray together, the goal of unity seems closer' (section 22).
- Discuss, dialogue and study together (section 28).
- Embrace every form of practical co-operation at all levels: pastoral, cultural, social, witness to the Gospel message. 'In the eyes of the world, co-operation among Christians becomes a form of common witness and a means of evangelisation which benefits all involved' (section 40).
- 'It is understandable how the seriousness of the commitment to ecumenism presents a deep challenge to the Catholic faithful. The Spirit calls them to make a serious examination of conscience' (section 82).

- The Catholic Church must enter into what might be called a 'dialogue of conversion' which constitutes the spiritual foundation of ecumenical dialogue. In this dialogue, which takes place before God, each individual must recognise his or her own faults, confess his or her sins, and place himself or herself in the hands of the One who is our intercessor before the Father – Jesus Christ' (section 82).
- 'How indeed can we proclaim the Gospel of reconciliation without at the same time being committed to working for reconciliation between Christians?' (section 98).
- 'The power of God's Spirit gives growth and builds up the Church. As the Church turns her gaze to the new millennium, she asks the Spirit for the grace to strengthen her own unity and to make it grow towards full communion with other Christians' (section 102).

In this Encyclical Letter, Pope (now Saint) John Paul II made absolutely clear his own conviction of the importance of all of us working together for much greater unity in the body of Christ.

THE CHARTA OECUMENICA OF 2001 –
AN IMPORTANT DOCUMENT

This Charta offers guidelines for the growing co-operation among the Churches in Europe, produced by the Catholic Council of European Bishops' Conferences and the Conference of European Churches.

'We commit ourselves to work in the power of the Holy Spirit towards the visible unity of the Church of Jesus Christ in the one faith, expressed in the mutual recognition of Baptism and in Eucharistic Fellowship, as well as in common witness and service.'

SOME EXAMPLES OF OUR SHARED HERITAGE:
- Our history
- The Bible
- Our Saviour
- The Trinity – Father, Son and Spirit
- A basic Creed
- Baptism
- Our Mission
- Eternal Life

SOME SCRIPTURES RELATING TO UNITY:
- Psalm 133
- 1 Corinthians 1:10
- Ephesians 4:1-6
- Matthew 12:26
- John 13:34-35
- John 15:9-17 and 17:20-26

FIVE POPES – THE UNFOLDING OF AN ECUMENICAL VISION

SAINT JOHN XXIII

As we have already said, **Pope Saint John XXIII** was determined to put Christian Unity firmly on the map and into the teaching of the Council. This determination had grown during his years serving as Papal Nuncio in a number of countries including Turkey, Bulgaria, Greece and France, and the result is that the Vatican II approach to ecumenism presented in **Unitatis Redintegratio** is entirely consistent with the vision contained in **Lumen Gentium, the Dogmatic Constitution on the Church**, in that the view of the people of God presented in chapter 2 of **Lumen Gentium** includes not only other Christians but also the Jews and members of other religions. This view is to some extent echoed in **section 22 of Gaudium et Spes** which also addresses the nature of the Church.

VATICAN II – ECUMENICAL DIALOGUE CENTRAL TO THE IDENTITY OF THE CATHOLIC CHURCH

In the introduction to the **Catholic Truth Society pamphlet 'The Gift of Dialogue'**, Archbishop Kevin McDonald explains the new approach in these words:-

'**At Vatican II the Church drew on Scripture and Tradition to set out a positive and theologically grounded vision of other Churches and Ecclesial Communities. The Council's teaching did this in such a way that ecumenical dialogue which seeks to establish ever fuller communion between separated Christians became central to the mission, and indeed, the identity of the Catholic Church.**'

POPE PAUL VI – THE PLACE OF DIALOGUE

Following this new approach of Vatican II, in 1964 Pope Paul VI wrote '**Ecclesiam Suam**' to guide this journey forward, which among other things described the important place of dialogue as *'originating in the mind of God himself and finding expression in prayer.'* It was becoming clear that dialogue expresses something which is at the heart of what the Church is all about.

After the Council was over, **Pope Paul VI** established what would later become **The Pontifical Council for Promoting Christian Unity**, which later resulted in our own Bishops' Conference of England and Wales taking up the challenge of promoting unity, and

later presenting the Council's teaching in '**One Bread, One Body'**
in 1998.

SAINT JOHN PAUL II

The whole Pontificate of John Paul II was characterised by an
ecumenical openness, with a number of significant contributions
to the development of closer relationships with both Orthodox and
Protestant leaders. A good example of this was his visit to the
United Kingdom and his time in Canterbury Cathedral with the
Archbishop. But as we have already seen, his sense of being called
to write **Ut Unum Sint** and the clear views he expressed in doing
this, provide an invaluable handbook for the development of our
ecumenical relationships. In **Tertio Millennio Adveniente,** section
16, he also reminded us: '**Among the most fervent petitions which
the Church makes to the Lord during this important time as the
new millennium approaches, is that unity among all Christians
of the various confessions will increase until they reach full
communion.**'

POPE BENEDICT XVI – HIS PRIMARY TASK

Rather surprisingly at the very beginning of his papacy, Pope
Benedict stated that re-building the full and visible unity of all
Christ's followers was his primary task. He said it was clear that
'**for Catholics, ecumenism is absolutely central to the Christian
life, both in terms of the Church becoming who she is and in
terms of the Church's mission.**' He said that in the end, each and
every Christian must come before Christ and '**render an account
to him of all we have done or failed to do to further the great good
of the full and visible unity of all his disciples.**'

POPE FRANCIS – 'THE CULTURE OF ENCOUNTER AND DIALOGUE'

With the election of Pope Francis, ecumenism has received a powerful impetus. In addition to developing strong personal relationships with Orthodox and main-line Protestant leaders, Pope Francis has brought with him from Argentina his experience of building close friendships and co-operation with Evangelical, Independent and Pentecostal leaders. One of the expectations Pope Francis has of the Charismatic Renewal is that we will witness to Spiritual Ecumenism with all those brothers and sisters of other Churches and Christian Communities who believe in Jesus as Lord and Saviour, remembering that the Charismatic Renewal is ecumenical by its very nature.

As **Cardinal Kurt Koch, President of the Pontifical Council for Promoting Christian Unity**, explains it, **Pope Francis'** approach to ecumenism is setting him apart from his predecessors including **Benedict XVI**. This is because Francis lays a greater emphasis on strengthening ecumenical relationships through praying together and doing things together, taking a realistic view that theological dialogue alone will not get us any further. Friendly relationships are an essential condition for even beginning to discuss difficult theological questions, according to Francis. If we are to be an evangelising Church taking the Gospel message all over the world, we need to do it together.

WORK TOGETHER NOW

Cardinal Koch says that for **Pope Francis** ecumenism has the highest priority and he continually emphasises that we must work together now – we cannot wait until we are one. We must walk along the same path, bear the same witness and pray together. **'Sisterliness and friendship between the different Christian**

Churches and church communities, as well as bearing witness, are very high priorities for Pope Francis', said Cardinal Koch.

NEW DOORS ARE BEING OPENED

He also explained that the emphasis in ecumenical dialogue seemed to be changing. Something is certainly changing in so far as new doors for dialogue are being opened, doors which have been closed up to now, and this is very significant. Relations with Pentecostals were becoming particularly important. He explained **'There were those among the Pentecostals and Evangelicals who were prejudiced against the Catholic Church and the papacy, but if these groups meet the Pope personally and see that he is a good Christian, it can overcome many prejudices and open doors for new dialogues. This is particularly important as Pentecostalism has become the second-largest reality in Christianity after the Catholic Church.'**

(**NB:** I personally think that here the Cardinal is linking the New Independent Charismatic Churches with the Pentecostals as one large grouping).

In 2005 Sue and I arranged to meet Cardinal Bergoglio (now Pope Francis) in Buenos Aires, and with our Catholic friends Kevin and Dorothy Ranaghan invited six Pentecostal and Protestant leaders to accompany us. Our purpose was to discuss with Cardinal Bergoglio the extremely positive and inter-active relationships he had established with key Pentecostal and Protestant leaders in Argentina. He happily shared his experience with us, asked us to pray over him, and assured us of the importance of what we were doing. You can imagine our delight when he was elected Pope!

AN ECUMENICAL GRACE

Among Francis' stated 'expectations' for the Catholic Charismatic

Renewal we find: '**Give witness of spiritual ecumenism with all those brothers and sisters of other Churches and Christian communities who believe in Jesus as Lord and Saviour. The Charismatic Renewal is by its very nature ecumenical.**' He clearly sees Renewal in the Spirit as an **ecumenical grace**, a view which echoes **Pope Saint John Paul II: '…by your experience of the many gifts of the Holy Spirit which are also shared with our separated brothers and sisters, yours is the special joy of growing in a desire for the unity to which the Spirit guides us and in a commitment to the serious work of ecumenism.**'

It's interesting to note that Pope Francis also believes that the Reformation was really over in 1999 when the Catholic Church and the Lutheran Church Federation issued a joint declaration on justification '**by God's grace through faith in Christ**'. This Declaration was adopted by the **World Methodist Council** in 2006.

WHAT LIES BEHIND THE REMARKABLY CLOSE RELATION-SHIPS POPE FRANCIS ENJOYS WITH EVANGELICALS AND PENTECOSTALS?

When he was in Argentina he saw Catholics leaving the Church to join the Evangelicals and Pentecostals, and as a traditional Jesuit this must have filled him with dismay. His initial encounter with the **Catholic Charismatic Renewal** was not promising – he described it as a '**samba dancing party**' – but as the Archbishop of Buenos Aires he started attending their noisy, praise-filled meetings and quickly changed his mind from this initial view. He also began to join evangelical meetings where he was prayed over and began to meet regularly with groups of evangelical pastors, enthusiastically joining in with their spontaneous prayer times. He clearly believes that our shared baptism and openness to the Holy Spirit is more important than our theological differences, leaving those to the theologians to solve. All this he shared with us in 2005. Since becoming Pope, Francis has continued to meet informally with Protestant and Pentecostal leaders on a regular basis, and in this **Bishop Tony Palmer** played a major part before his untimely death in a motor cycle accident. Francis often speaks of '**receptive ecumenism**', firm in his conviction that we all have gifts we are called to share with each other.

ANNIVERSARY CELEBRATIONS – 1967 TO 2017 50 YEARS OF CATHOLIC RENEWAL

At the **50th Anniversary Celebrations of the Catholic Charismatic Renewal in 2017**, Pope Francis was insistent that leaders from all the other Charismatic Churches would be there as of right, not just because we invited them, and on the platform on the eve of **Pentecost** in the **Circus Maximus** they were seated in the row behind him. Alongside him in the front row were **Fr. Raniero Cantalamessa** the Papal Preacher and **Pentecostal Pastor Giovanni Traettino**, who were both speakers at the invitation of Francis. Patti Mansfield from the 1967 Duquesne Weekend and Michelle Moran, past President of ICCRS, were seated alongside him. Sue and I were up there too, because Francis said we were a good visual example of an ecumenical marriage!

WHERE IS ALL THIS LEADING US?

It's difficult to say. Certainly Francis is doing a lot:
- encouraging Catholics to be more evangelical and to preach the Gospel everywhere;
- he's supporting much closer Catholic relationships with the Pentecostals and Independent Charismatic churches and fellowships;
- he's tackling the deep distrust of Catholics still prevalent in many evangelical circles;

- he's using a new terminology: social friendship, spiritual ecumenism (from Vatican II), reconciled diversity, unity without uniformity, the culture of encounter and dialogue – all expressing and promoting his new approach to relations with a section of Christianity which, with the exception of the Catholic Charismatics, was outside the experience of most normal Catholics. As such I firmly believe we are called to support him in every way we can.

FROM CONFLICT TO COMMITMENT - THE 'C' SCALE

I cannot remember if I wrote/adapted this or if I found it somewhere in this form, but... as Christians we often follow a process in which we move from:-

- **Conflict to Competition**
- **Competition to Co-existence**
- **Co-existence to Co-operation**
- **Co-operation to Commitment**
- **And one day, please God, we'll move from Commitment to Communion**

It can be helpful to identify where our local churches are on this scale, and as many of us are already enjoying a remarkable level of commitment to each other, we need to celebrate this.

SOME PRINCIPLES OF CHRISTIAN UNITY – A PERSONAL VIEW

The commitment to work for the unity of all Christians is a special calling for many of us in the **Catholic Charismatic Renewal**. Our shared experience of **Baptism in the Holy Spirit** has made a bridge between us and many of our Protestant, Independent and Pentecostal brothers and sisters.

On our journey towards full communion, **Pope Saint John Paul II** emphasised in **Ut Unum Sint** the importance of praying, discussing, co-operating and giving joint witness with those from other ecclesial communities. But at the same time we do need to be alert to the dangers of a false ecumenism which pretends there are really no differences between us.

So here I want to offer some simple principles to guide us in our important ecumenical work and to ensure we avoid the dangers of a false approach to this important topic.

1. Accept one another as brothers and sisters in Christ.
The Church reminds us that through our shared baptism we are already in relationship and we need to recognise this and banish the old stereotypes, stopping criticising each other.

2. Be faithful to who you are, sure about your Church teaching.
We need to know why we are Catholic, what we believe, and be faithful to it. Whilst we accept that all those who are justified by faith and incorporated into Christ by baptism are to be properly regarded as our brothers and sisters, we also believe that Christianity is to be found in its fullness in the Catholic Church.

3. Remember that while there are important differences between us, more unites us than separates us.
Whilst we cannot pretend that important differences do not exist or do not matter, we should begin by concentrating on those things on which we agree – they are many! Sometimes the problem is that we have a different way of saying the same things, so let's always look at what is meant rather than at how it is expressed.

4. Repent together for our differences – forgive and ask forgiveness.

Examining our hearts, recognising our faults and seeking forgiveness from the Lord and from each other presents a deep challenge to all of us (Ut Unum Sint section 82).

5. Listen and learn what others believe and why.

No relationship will grow unless both parties are willing to listen. Listening shows respect and helps us to understand why others have different beliefs. We don't have to agree with them but it's important that we understand them.

6. Build and protect personal relationships.

We need to get to know each other well, to support and encourage one another, and to stand up for each other when we are attacked by those opposed to what we are doing.

7. Accept that there is a healthy tension between Love and Truth, but remember that Love is the authentic sign of true Christianity.

We will not make any progress without love, because only in love can we together search for the truth, and the degree to which we can be seen to love one another is a sign of our progress.

8. Recognise that there's a price to be paid when working for unity.

There will be many difficulties and misunderstandings on the journey. At times it will be very painful, we'll feel like turning back. We must accept that there's a price to be paid.

9. Do together as much as we can in good conscience, thereby giving public witness to our shared faith; never forgetting that Jesus prayed for unity among his followers.

We are called to 'every possible form of practical co-operation at all levels: pastoral, cultural and social, as well as that of witnessing to the Gospel message', (Ut Unum Sint section 40). So we must pray as if it all depends on God, whilst working together as if it all depends on us.

10 . Finally, never forget that Jesus and the Father want unity, and that it is a work of the Holy Spirit.
So prayer remains the most important activity. As we pray together our respect for one another grows, as does our shared concern for unity. From this will flow true ecumenical co-operation in the areas of promoting Gospel values, meeting needs, challenging injustice, and demonstrating mutual respect with a willingness to listen and to dialogue. Then the witness we give will speak loudly to the society in which we live and will support our shared proclamation of the basic Gospel message.

So pray as if it all depends on God and work as if it all depends on you! We are not responsible for the actions and re-actions of other people but we are responsible for our own actions and reactions. We must each do everything we can for Christian unity under the guidance of the Holy Spirit and in accordance with the teaching of the Church,which clearly exhorts us to take an active and intelligent part in this essential work.

HOW DO WE DO THIS?
- by building good relationships with the members of the other Christian churches and fellowships in our area.
- by getting to know, appreciate and respect one another
- by praying and sharing together on a regular basis
- by doing together as much as we possibly can
- by loving one another as brothers and sisters in Christ

- by praying for a new outpouring of the Holy Spirit on us all
- by joyfully celebrating together the amazing grace of salvation in Jesus Christ that we all share

SOME PERSONAL NOTES

BACKGROUND

My mother was a strong Catholic, my father a middle-of-the-road Anglican. I was born in 1942 in World War II, my father was serving in the British army and for four years I was brought up by my mother until my father returned. We went to Mass together and at the age of nine I went away to a Jesuit boarding school. I developed a strong intellectual understanding of my Catholic faith, but it didn't really touch my heart.

After school I went to Durham University where I met Sue, an atheist, and we were married the year after we left university. I went to Mass on an intermittent basis, and my atheist wife often came with me, particularly after we had our first two children. We had been married ten years when we were persuaded to join an Anglican, Baptist and Catholic discussion group to look at our Christian faith together. Sue was warmly included even though she had given up her traditional Anglican faith in her teenage years. For the first time we both encountered Christians whose faith was alive and on fire, and who talked about their living faith in Jesus and the empowerment of the Holy Spirit.

All this resulted in Sue giving her life to the Lord, and my faith coming alive some months later through the prophetic inspiration of an Anglican priest, who prayed for me. The ecumenical witness of the other members of the discussion group was so strong in all this that a passionate desire to work together in unity was birthed in us both. When we then prayerfully asked the Lord where he wanted us to worship, he said to us both quite independently 'bloom where you were planted'. So I have remained Catholic and Sue Anglican, the Church of her childhood. We go to Mass together on Sundays when Sue receives a prayer of blessing, and to an Anglican communion service on Wednesdays, when I receive a prayer of blessing. Since our faith came alive in 1976 we have worked to build loving relationships and greater mutual understanding throughout the body of Christ, whilst remaining faithful and active in our respective denominations.

WORKING FOR UNITY - WHAT DOES THIS MEAN IN PRACTICE?

For 30 years, between 1978 and 2008, we held a **weekly ecumenical prayer meeting** at home. We travel together in the UK and all over the world giving talks at conferences and in churches of different denominations.

Since 2000 I have chaired the ecumenical **International Charismatic Consultation on World Evangelisation**, and with Hugh Osgood I co-chair the **Charismatic and Pentecostal Leaders Annual Conference** in the UK. I also co-chair the ecumenical international 'Gatherings in the Holy Spirit' which take place in Rome every second year involving **Catholic Charismatic leaders** and **Independent Charismatic leaders**, and which have given birth to conversations between six of the **Independent leaders** and the **Pontifical Council for Promoting Christian Unity**. In 2003 I was invited to join the **Azusa Street Centennial Cabinet** as the only non-Pentecostal member, to plan and organise the events in Los Angeles to celebrate the 100 years anniversary of Pentecostalism in

April 2006. They told me I was there as the representative of the rest of world Christianity! It was a great honour and privilege.

I was for 10 years a Director of **Premier Christian Radio and Media**, and I am currently a Director and Trustee of **The Christian Healing Mission** based in West London. Both organisations are strongly committed to the search for Christian Unity.

INTERNATIONAL, NATIONAL AND LOCAL

As a Catholic, between 1989 and 1999 I chaired the **International Catholic Charismatic Renewal Council (ICCRS)**, with an office in the Vatican and regular meetings with Pope St. John Paul II. I served as Chairman of our **National Catholic Charismatic Renewal Service Committee in England** for 20 years, and was then elected a life member. Today I am a member of my **Diocesan Ecumenical Commission and a Trustee and Director of my Catholic Diocese of Northampton**. I am also active in my parish, which I have served in many different capacities over the years, including three stints as **Chair of the Parish Council.**

Locally I chaired **The Big Tent Event** in 1991, a two week long ecumenical joint mission presented by all the Christian Churches together in our area (Baptist, Catholic, Methodist, United Reformed and three Anglican churches) and since 1991 I have hosted a **monthly prayer meeting** for all the local ministers, priests, vicars, curates and pastors. We also share a two day **Retreat** together every year. I believe it's vital to develop strong relationships between local churches of every persuasion. Our loving relationships have resulted in many shared local initiatives to present the Gospel message together and to build faith among us. We offer joint ALPHA courses, and on special occasions go onto the streets of our village together to give witness to our faith in a variety of ways. In order to build up more prayer for our area in our respective congregations, about 2 years ago we opened a 24/7 Prayer Room in the centre of our village, in which every local church is involved.

I hope the above gives some flavour of what lies behind my strong desire to write this short booklet '**Love One Another**' and will help the reader to understand my views a little better and why unity is so important to me.

Some years ago I wrote a pamphlet entitled '**What is the nature of the Catholic Charismatic Renewal**?' published by Good News Publications, PO Box 67138, London SW11 9FD, and I have written two books '**Pentecost Is Always for Living**' and '**Towards A Fuller Life In The Holy Spirit**'. Both have been translated into a number of languages and the English versions are available from New Life Publishing, Luton, LU4 9HG, UK.

In all of this, over more than forty years, the desire to see an ever-increasing unity throughout the whole body of Christ locally, nationally, and internationally, remains of paramount importance in my local work. For all of us this begins with the building of strong personal relationships where we live with our Christian brothers and sisters from other expressions of the body of Christ. Little of substance will happen ecumenically until these relationships are in place and we are regularly meeting to pray together.

© J. Charles Whitehead, KSG
Holly Trees, Bull Lane, Chalfont St. Peter,
Bucks, SL9 8RZ. UK
email: whiteheadchas@aol.com
Tel: +44 (0)1753 883971 & 07720 808890   January 2019

Further copies of this booklet and
two other books from Charles Whitehead:
Pentecost is Always for Living, and
Towards a Fuller Life in the Holy Spirit
can be obtained from

Goodnews Books, Upper level
St. John's Church Complex
296 Sundon Park Road
Luton, Beds. LU3 3AL

www.goodnewsbooks.co.uk
orders@goodnewsbooks.co.uk
01582 571011

Pope Francis encourages us all to be involved in 'spiritual ecumenism', and has said he is not thinking about doctrinal agreements but about the need to build strong personal relationships with all our Christian brothers and sisters.

For him, relationships come first and are more important than our theological differences.
'Love One Another' puts his views into the wider context of Church teaching from the time of the Second Vatican Council, 1962-1964, up to today.

'In this booklet, Charles Whitehead reminds us of some of the Church's key teachings about ecumenism, and reading through them one has to wonder how much this teaching has really been appreciated and implemented'.
+Kevin Mcdonald, Archbishop Emeritus, Southwark
(taken from his Foreword)

NEW LIFE

9 781912 237166
ISBN 978 1 912237 16 6